LACOCK

An illustrated souvenir

The National Trust

Lacock

Lacock, with its grid of four streets, remains today much as it looked in the eighteenth century. The lively town of two hundred years ago, with its crowded market thronged with pedlars and sideshows, animals and poultry abutting the more sedate everyday shops and businesses, can still be imagined. Nowadays, Lacock is filled with a different kind of bustle – the crowds of visitors come year after year but it is to admire its architecture, with houses of every century from the thirteenth onwards, and to enjoy the tranquil atmosphere of a living village able to recapture the spirit of the past.

Between the village and the River Avon lies the meadow of Snaylesmeade on which stands Lacock Abbey. This thirteenth-century nunnery was converted into a house at the Dissolution of the Monasteries in Henry VIII's reign. It contains fine examples of medieval, Tudor and eighteenth-century building. Lacock is also well known as the home of photography. William Henry Fox Talbot, the inventor of the negative, lived at Lacock Abbey and his earliest surviving negative was of a window in the house.

The owners of the Abbey were landlords of the village. As a nunnery, it had a high reputation for care of the villagers' needs and this was perpetuated by the secular landlords, first the Sharington family and then through marriage, the Talbots. Miss Matilda Talbot gave her property in Lacock to the National Trust in 1944, and though the surname has changed, the Trust's tenants in the Abbey are descendants of the family.

Weathered stone roof tiles, encrusted with lichen and covered with stonecrop and moss.

An aerial view of the village looking east. The Abbey can be seen at the top right, while the course of the Bide Brook is clearly marked as it runs north of Church Street into the Avon at the top left.

The Origins of Lacock

Lacock lies in a part of the country that has attracted settlers from the earliest times. An Iron Age camp lies at the top of Naish Hill a mile or two from Lacock and a Roman road ran about half a mile to the south of the village. Probably the earliest permanent inhabitants were the Saxons who lived by the Bide Brook which flows through the middle of the village; they called it 'lacuc' meaning little stream. The River Avon nearby was important both for communication and fish.

In the Domesday Book Lacock is mentioned as belonging to Edward of Salisbury, Sheriff of Wiltshire, the son of one of William the Conqueror's knights. It is described thus: '. . . *there are twelve villeins and sixteen cossets with three cottars. There are two mills paying seventeen shillings and sixpence, and twenty acres of meadow and half an acre of vineyard. The wood is one mile between length and breadth. It was and is worth £7.'* One of the mills is thought to be Rey Mill which was in use until well into this century.

The early village was bounded on the south by Melksham Forest, one of the royal hunting forests. The neighbouring manor of Lackham was held by William de Ow, and there is a record that he entertained the king and a considerable court '*at his manor at Lacock*' in 1086. Parts of King John's Hunting Lodge beside the church date back to the thirteenth century. Built where it is, the house would certainly have belonged to one of the more important people in the village, and it is quite possible that the king stayed here on his hunting trips in the Forest.

The 18th-century packhorse bridge over the Bide Brook. The Saxons called it 'lacuc', little stream, and settled nearby. In the foreground is the ford.

The Foundation of the Abbey

Lacock Abbey was founded in the early thirteenth century by Ela, Countess of Salisbury. Ela was the daughter of Patrick, Earl of Salisbury, and great-granddaughter of Edward who held Lacock at the time of Domesday. She was married to William Longespee, the illegitimate son of Henry II. William was one of the most powerful barons of the time. He was a witness of Magna Carta and with Ela laid the fourth and fifth foundation stones of Salisbury Cathedral. Ela founded two religious houses in his memory on the same day, involving a journey of sixteen miles, the one at Hinton Charterhouse for Carthusian monks and the other at Lacock for Augustinian canonesses.

The Abbey was built with stone obtained from Ralph Croc, who owned the quarry at Hazelbury near Box, and with timbers from the royal forest – in 1248 Henry III made a grant of four oaks from the forest of Chippenham and fifteen from the royal forests, and later. Edward I made a grant of ten oaks from Melksham Forest. The Crown continued this support, assisting with the repair of a granary struck by lightning in 1447 and granting enclosure of forty acres of woodland for the nuns' sole use in the forest. Generally, the Abbey prospered throughout the Middle Ages. The rich farmlands of its endowment by Ela ensured a sizeable income from wool throughout its medieval life. The nuns were mostly ladies of good family, usually between fifteen and twenty-five in number but the community was increased by a number of lay sisters, who looked after the more menial tasks, and guests who came for hospitality.

Part of the 15th-century Cloisters, with the bright sunlight casting the shadows of the window tracery on the opposite wall.

Left Some of the Abbey's fine collection of decorative tiles.

The Chapter House, opening on to the Cloisters, was the formal meeting place where the day-to-day affairs of the nunnery were discussed. The floor tiles are 19th-century.

Lacock Abbey and the Medieval Village

The poor people of Lacock benefited from having the Abbey in the village. In the thirteenth century it gave a daily dole to one destitute person throughout the year and to three during Lent. On Maundy Thursday both food and money were dispensed to the needy and on Good Friday twenty-two loaves distributed. Just before the Dissolution it was described as *'of great and large buildings set in a towne. To the same . . . by common reporte a great releef.'*

Most of the inhabitants of Lacock were tenants of the Abbey. Although they were obliged to perform various services on the manor lands in return for their holdings – sowing and spreading dung for instance – they might receive the right to dine *'at the lady's table'* on certain days or were granted the milk from one cow for eight days. They paid their rents in kind: corn, hides, fleeces were collected in the fine fourteenth-century tithe barn. This is a cruck beam construction of which there are several other noteworthy examples in the village, particularly Cruck House in Church Street, where the beam is shown exposed. The Chamberlain's House at the corner of the High and East Streets was very likely the residence of some official connected with the Abbey.

Timber, stone and brick are combined in the 14th-century Cruck House on the corner of Church Street. Not only is this house one of the earliest in Lacock, but its cruck construction (an exposed cruck can be clearly seen) is a rare example in south England.

The massive timbers of the 14th-century tithe barn on the corner of East Street and High Street, rise above a simple beaten earth floor. Later the barn became the market hall, and later still it stored grain for a threshing machine which stood in the doorway.

Industries

During the Middle Ages Lacock became a prosperous and thriving town through its wool industry. Sheep grazed on the nearby downs and the village was well placed for communications, sited as it was on the 'cloth road' from London (the present road down Bowden Hill) and the River Avon, which gave access to the sea at Avonmouth near Bristol.

In the fifteenth century broad looms were introduced and many houses were built with wide first-floor rooms to accommodate them. Even today the High Street shows this very clearly.

The size of many dwellings bears witness to the wealth of the inhabitants. Some retain their horse passages. These allowed the animal to be led from the street to the stabling in the backyard.

The horse passage of the 'The Angel' through which horses were led from Church Street to the yard behind.

Church Street, looking west, with Cruck House half-closing the vista, and 'The Sign of The Angel', bright with flowers, on the right.

The jettied first storey of this half-timbered house in Church Street once accommodated a hand loom.

Lacock Church

No sign remains of a possible Saxon church at Lacock. Moreover, there is no substantial architectural evidence for a Norman church, though the dedication to Cyriac is frequently found in Normandy, but is most unusual in this country. St Cyriac was a child martyr at the time of the persecutions of the Emperor Diocletian in the third century.

As it stands now, the church is mainly fifteenth-century when the village was at its prime, but there are traces of earlier work in the north transept, and one stone of an early arch can be seen in the chancel beside the organ loft. A 'squint' still remains between the north transept and the Lady Chapel.

Two features of the church are the unusually high arches of the nave and the very fine boarded waggon roof. Moreover, it abounds in stone carvings of all kinds – animals and humans – one of the most interesting being a man smoking a pipe before the introduction of tobacco, probably herbs of some sort, and one of the most amusing being the head-over-heels caper of a mischievous urchin.

Two handsome memorials to the various families who lived at Lackham can be found in the south transept. One brass, dated 1501, is dedicated to Robert Baynard, his wife, five sons and thirteen daughters. One of the latter was mother of the last Abbess at the Abbey. Across the nave in the Lady Chapel stands the magnificent tomb to Sir William Sharington, the first lay owner of the Abbey.

The church from the west. The tower was built in the 16th century, later than most of the building.

This sturdy sheepgate allowed access to the public but safeguarded the churchyard from voracious invaders.

The Reformation and Sir William Sharington

The price paid by Sir William Sharington for Lacock Abbey, land and buildings, on its dissolution in 1539, was £783. Sharington, from a wealthy Norfolk family, held various positions at court and was knighted at the coronation of Edward VI. However, intrigue and nefarious dealings with the coinage in collusion with Lord Thomas Seymour, Treasurer of the Mint, led to their arrest in 1549. Sharington confessed, blamed Seymour who was beheaded, but escaped himself with an attainder and forfeit of lands. Sometime later on payment of the large sum of £8,000 he regained all his land, including Lacock.

Sharington possessed excellent artistic taste, influenced by an early visit to Italy. In converting the nunnery he retained much medieval work. He built the octagonal tower of three storeys at the south-east corner of the cloisters and the bizarre Renaissance chimneys piercing the skyline; also, in domestic vein, the stable court to the north which houses the bakehouse, brewery and stables.

Sir William Sharington had no children and was followed at Lacock by his brother, Sir Henry Sharington, who entertained Queen Elizabeth to a meal and was knighted by her. Henry's youngest daughter, Olive, married Sir John Talbot of Salwarp in Worcestershire, and this family has been connected with the Abbey ever since.

The portrait of Sir William Sharington in the South Gallery in the Abbey.

The pleasing asymmetry of Sharington's Stable Court, which tradition says was built with materials from the demolished Abbey Church.

The ornate Renaissance tomb of Sir William Sharington (d. 1553), the first lay owner of the Abbey.

The Avon flowing through 'Snaylesmeade' beside the east front of the Abbey.

The Talbots

During the Civil War, the Talbot family supported the Royalist cause and a garrison was quartered at the Abbey. However, it proved unsuitable as a fortified house, surrendered to General Fairfax, and Parliamentary troops ensconced themselves. Sharington Talbot was fined £1,100 for his allegiance to the Stuarts but his son, John, was knighted at the Restoration.

John Ivory Talbot, great-grandson of the above, was a Member of Parliament for Wiltshire and a Doctor of Civil Law at Oxford University. His sixty-year span at Lacock saw extensive alterations to the Abbey and grounds. Parkland replaced elaborately laid out gardens, and the line of the drive was altered to make a carriage sweep before the front door, approached through a Gothick arch. Two chimneys from the east of the house were placed beside the drive with a figure of a sphinx resting on them.

Most important of all, Talbot created the large Gothick entrance hall, replacing an earlier Tudor or medieval hall. Built in 1754–6 to the design of Sanderson Miller, it is one of the earliest examples in the country of the Gothick. Approached up a double flight of steps, inside it has an arresting ceiling bearing the coats of arms of neighbouring families. The walls are decorated with terracotta statues by the Austrian craftsman, Victor Alexander Sederbach.

One of Sederbach's terracotta figures over the fireplace in the Hall.

The portrait of John Ivory Talbot (d. 1772) by Michael Dahl, which hangs in the Stone Gallery.

John Ivory Talbot, delighted with his new Hall, wrote to Sanderson Miller about its opening, '*when all my friends who are in the country and whose arms are emblazoned on the ceiling will do me the honour of their company and a grand sacrifice to Bacchus will be the consequence.*'

Communications

Changes at the Abbey were shadowed in the village. The elegant brick facade of Cantax House was added in the early eighteenth century, whilst the more strident statement of bricks on the High Street front of the Red Lion dates from 1740, in both instances shielding buildings of an earlier era.

The London to Bath road was turnpiked in 1713 but enjoyed only a brief heyday before the advent of the new road with gentler gradients through Chippenham. Within the village a Mr Dummer built the small packhorse bridge which crosses the Bide Brook beside the ford. In 1935 the walls of this bridge were washed away by a disastrous flood and were rebuilt by the local stonemason.

Transport of stone from the Corsham quarries to London was much eased with the opening of a branch of the Kennet and Avon Canal, running east of the River Avon. This linked Devizes and Abingdon, and joined the North Wiltshire Canal at Swindon. Names such as The Wharf and Toll Cottage recall the years between 1810 and 1900 when waterborne traffic was at its busiest, but by the outbreak of war in 1914 the canal branch had been abandoned and today only a slight depression in the fields traces its bed.

The bed of the old Wiltshire and Berkshire Canal, running east of the Avon, is now grassed over, and only the willows stand sentinel along its former banks.

Cantax House was the vicarage from the early 17th century until 1865, when a new vicarage was built at the top of Cantax Hill, leading north-west out of the village.

Inns and Hostelries

The oldest inn is The George in West Street which holds one of the longest continuously held licences in the West Country. Known for many centuries as The Inn, it was renamed at the time of King George II. This was a fashionable title at a time when popular imagination was fired by George II, the last English king to lead his subjects into battle.

In 1656 two blasphemers were arraigned before the Grand Jury after airing their views over a pint of ale at The Inn. William Bond (weaver) affirmed '*that there was noe god or power only above the Planetts. And that there was noe Christ but the son that shines upon us*' and Thomas Hibberd (weaver) that '*he did believe that god was in all things and if hee was drunk* (meaning the said Thomas Hibberd) *god was drunke with him. . .*'. The sentence passed is not recorded.

At the time of Edward IV, when the wool trade was flourishing, the inn, The Angel, in Church Street was built. It was named after the gold coin called an angel, not an allusion to a heavenly body. It is a timber-framed building with much internal panelling and it boasts one of the finest horse passages in the village.

Sir William Sharington's sixteenth-century brewery remains in the Abbey courtyard. As with all working buildings, it must have been altered substantially from the original but survived at least two hundred years of hard use. The mash tun where the ingredients were heated, the cooling trough and the fermenting vat still stand.

The imposing brick facade of the 'Red Lion', in High Street, was built about 1740 but conceals a much older building.

The George Inn, in West Street, the oldest hostelry in the village.

Part of the equipment of the Abbey's 16th-century brewery, probably in use until the 18th century.

In and out of work

The wool trade in Lacock came to an end with its general decline in the West Country during the Industrial Revolution, but other industries were more buoyant. One of the foremost was the tannery, which closed only in 1928. The area behind the church is still known as the Tanyard. Skins were washed in the brook nearby and dried in the big open barn behind the church, and oak and ash bark were collected by boys in the village.

Near the site of the old tannery stands the nineteenth-century workhouse, built in the 1830s to cope with the indigent and infirm. The early years of this decade must have been a lean time for the villagers. A party of twenty emigrated in *The Wilson* to Canada in 1832, funded by the local inhabitants at a cost of £240. Employment on the Chippenham railway relieved the situation by the 1840s when the workhouse was 'home' to 146 labourers on the line.

In contrast to the gaunt workhouse, the neat squat dimensions of the eighteenth-century lock-up or blind house in East Street provided punishment of a short sharp incarceration in pitch darkness for the drunk and disorderly. (The enduring tradition of working with stone in the village was demonstrated by the local mason's ability to repair the roof in the 1950s without the use of scientific instruments.)

The Lacock page in the 1840 Post Office Directory reveals a lively village existence.

The gaunt Workhouse, behind the church and next to the Tanyard, closed in 1861, is now softened by shrubs and flowers and occupied by a potter. The Tanyard, where oak, ash and elm bark was dried, is a reminder of a thriving Lacock industry.

Wiltshire Friendly Society (branch of), held at the National school-room. Nights for meeting, first monday after each quarter-day, William Wright, steward National School, William Wright, master; Miss Patience Brockway, mistress [school-room There is a lending library for the parish at the National

West Knoyle.
Carlew Rev. James Walker [vicar]
Carey Alfred, dairyman

Mead John, parish clerk
Mitchell John, farmer
Rumsey John, farmer

Rumsey William, farmer
Letters have to be sent for to Mere

LACOCK, with
Hamlets of BOWDEN HILL and NOTTON.
LACOCK, or Laycock, is a parish and village, formerly a market-town, distant 4 miles north of Melksham, 3 miles south-east from Corsham, 3 miles south of Chippenham, 12½ miles east of Bath, 32 miles north of Salisbury, and 96 miles from London, in the Hundred of Chippenham, on the river Avon. The living is a vicarage, value £325, in the gift of W. H. Fox Talbot, Esq., of Lacock Abbey; the Rev. James Paley, M.A., is the present incumbent; the Rev. John Mathews, M.A., is the curate. The church is an ancient structure, in good repair, in the Gothic style of architecture, with a spire, containing 6 bells. Here is an Independent chapel, a National school for boys and girls. Lacock Abbey was formerly a nunnery, founded by

Ela, Countess of Salisbury, about the year 1232. The principal seats are—T. H. S. Sotheron's, Esq., Bowden House; Capt. Rooke's, Lackham House; Sir J. Awdry's, Knt., Notton House; and H. G. Awdry's, Esq., Notton Lodge. The population of Lacock, including the hamlets of Bowden Hill and Notton, in 1841, was 1,709; containing 4,000 acres. W. H. F. Talbot, Esq., is lord of the manor. The Berks and Wilts canal runs near Lacock.
BOWDEN HILL is a hamlet in the parish of Lacock, distant 1½ miles east of that place, 5½ miles east-by-south of Chippenham, and 99½ miles from London.
NOTTON is a hamlet in the parish of Lacock, distant 1 mile north of that place, 3 miles south of Chippenham, and 1 mile from Corsham station.

Lacock.
GENTRY.
Barton Mrs. Catherine
Cullen Rev. James Edward
Mathews Rev. John, M.A. [curate]
Pearce Mrs. Sarah
Ridler Miss, Ragbridge cottage
Rooke Capt. Fredk. Wm. Lackham ho
Talbot William Henry Fox, esq. Lacock abbey
Tanner Miss Mary
TRADERS.
Banks George, coal merchant & mason
Banks John, Red Lion inn, & farmer
Barton Edmund, maltster & miller
Barton John, grocer, baker & butcher
Barton Richard, maltster, brewer, & hop merchant
Bath Thomas, baker
Blackham James, Angel inn

National School, John Simcoe, master; Miss Mary Carey, mistress

Bowden Hill.
Sotheron Thomas Henry Sutton, esq. M.P. for North Wilts
TRADERS.
Hayes William, beer retailer

Breach James, farmer, Wick farm
Brinkworth John, Carpenters' Arms inn, baker, & coal merchant
Carey George, plasterer & tiler
Clark David, farmer, White Hall farm
Cole Isaac, beer retailer, Raybridge
Cradock Miss Juliet, farmer, Catridge fm
Croker Joseph, farmer, Nash Hill farm
Curnick Robert, farmer, New farm
Fry Mrs. Hannah, farmer, Abbey farm
Fry Joseph, butcher
Fortnee Isaac, plumber & glazier
Fussell James, farmer, Stroud farm
Gale John, wheelwright & carpenter
Gerrish John, boot & shoe maker
Hutchins Thomas, miller, Arnold's mill
Jennings Joseph, surgeon
Knott Joseph, George inn
Lovell Edmund, relieving officer to the Chippenham union

Howell William, farmer, Arnold's farm
Letters are received through Chippenham

Notton.
Awdry Sir John Wither, knt. Notton ho

Knott Richard, carrier
Milson John, farmer
Milson William, farmer, Bewley Ct. fm
Moore Thomas, saddler & harness ma
Newman Miss Hannah, grocer
Oakeford John, tailor
Perkins Miss Catherine, schoolmistress
Phelps John, ironmonger & blacksmith
Pulling George, boot & shoe maker
Ring Mrs. Betty, blacksmith
Running Thomas, farmer, Showell fm
Smart Jacob, chairmaker, Raybridge
Smart Joseph, parish clerk
Snozell John, beer retailer & coal mer
Tanner Alfred, grocer & draper
Wheeler Mathew, farmer, Cuckoo Bush farm
Letters arrive from Chippenham 4 a.m. delivered ½ past 7 a.m. dispatched ½ past 10 p.m

Awdry Henry Goddard, esq. Notton ldg
Fussell Mr. Stephen
Sargent Mrs. Eleanor, farmer
Letters are received through the Chippenham office

CARRIER.—Richard Knott, to Bath, on sat. returning same day

CARRIERS TO SHAFTESBURY—Edward Crickmay & Co. from Hindon, calling at the 'Seymour Arms,' sat. returning same day. Thomas Snook, sat. & to Salisbury, tues, returning same days; Dyer, from Longbridge Deverill, calling at the 'Seymour Arms,' sat. returning same day

---

LANDFORD is a parish in the Hundred of Frustfield and Alderbury Union, situated on a branch of the river Test and borders of Hampshire, 10 miles south-east from Salisbury, and 7 west from Romsey, and contained, in 1841, 255 inhabitants. The living is a rectory, in the archdeaconry

GENTRY.
Bodmin William, esq
Girdlestone Rev. Henry, M.A
Trollope Capt. Wm. Henry, Landford ho

Allen Mrs. Ann, farmer
Andrews Reuben, farmer
Harrison James, painter & plumber
King Charles, shopkeeper

King Mrs. Mary, farmer
Knobbs John, master of National school
Moody Daniel, farmer
Letters received through Salisbury

and diocese of Salisbury, value £199, and in the patronage of Earl Nelson. The Rev. Henry Girdlestone, M.A., is the present incumbent. The church, dedicated to St. Andrew, presents nothing worthy of notice. Here is a small National school.

STEEPLE LANGFORD, HANGING LANGFORD, BATHAMPTON, and LITTLE LANGFORD.
STEEPLE LANGFORD, with HANGING LANGFORD, and BATHAMPTON is a village 9 miles west of Salisbury, 91 from London by the old road, in the Hundred of Branch and Dole, and Wilton Union. Lord Ashburton is lord of the manor. The church is in the early English style, with square tower and 5 bells. The living is a rectory, value 45s. 2r. 7p. of glebe land, about £600; the Rev. Robert T. Coates, M.A., is the incumbent; Rev. Peter

Blackbourne, M.A., curate. It is in the gift of Corpus Christi College; the acreage of the parish is 3,425 acres.
LITTLE LANGFORD is a village 9 miles west of Salisbury, 93 from London, in the Hundred of Branch and Dole; the population is very small, only 42; acreage, 950. Earl of Pembroke lord of the manor. The living is a rectory, in the gift of the Earl of Pembroke; the Rev. John Phelps, M.A., is the incumbent. The church is dedicated to St. Nicholas, and is built in a cruciform shape, a mixed style of architecture, and has but 1 bell.

Steeple Langford.
Blackburne Rev. Peter, M.A
TRADERS.
Doughty Daniel, miller
Doughty Frederick, carrier
Dredge Solomon, farmer
Giles James, harness maker
Newbury Mary, post office

Swayne John, farmer
Swayne Thomas, farmer

Hanging Langford.
TRADERS.
Ford James, shopkeeper
Giles George, farmer
Porrell Thomas, farmer

Bathampton.
Jarratt Herbert N. esq
Porrell Alfred, farmer
Read John, farmer

Little Langford.
Phelps Rev. John, M.A. The Rectory
Chapman Robert Styles, farmer
Letters received through Wilton

POST OFFICE.—Mary Newbury, receiver. Letters arrive from Heytesbury ½ p. 10 a.m. dispatched at 3 p.m

CARRIER TO SALISBURY—Fredk. Doughty, tues. & fri

Schooling

Education was provided prior to the opening of the village school. In 1818 a voluntary subscription school had a dozen pupils and about the same time there was a Sunday School of about 200 which met in a building in the garden of King John's Hunting Lodge.

Lacock School was intended to mark William Henry Fox Talbot's twenty-first birthday in 1821. But there was a delay of three years in building it, as some cottages had to be demolished and the cottagers rehoused. The number of pupils grew and at one time they overflowed. One hundred and twenty were taught in the school and sixty infants in the house opposite, which is now one of the village shops.

After school, Lacock's situation in the midst of rich farmland offered employment at three farms within the village itself – one in Red Lion Yard, Mill Farm beside Cantax House, and Manor Farm – and several more on the parish boundary. Chair-making, with local wood for the frames and dried rushes from the river, tightly plaited, for the seats, was another occupation, and hurdle-making also flourished. Carpenters, wheelwrights, a coal merchant, millers and bakers, and two blacksmiths provided a wealth of services at the turn of this century for which the village now has to look much further afield.

The town clock, near the National Trust Shop in High Street, dates from Queen Victoria's Golden Jubilee.

The old Market Cross stands in the playground of the village school, which stands back a little from High Street. The cross once stood outside the 'Red Lion'.

William Henry Fox Talbot

Lacock is widely known and visited as the home of photography. Lacock Abbey was the family home of William Henry Fox Talbot, the inventor of the negative-positive process. Although he was not born in Lacock, and did not come to live there until 1827, he conducted many of his early experiments at the Abbey and his earliest surviving negative, taken in 1835, is of an oriel window in the South Gallery. Many of his early photographs are delightful studies of family and domestic life at the Abbey, and several of these appear in his publication *The Pencil of Nature* – the first published book to be illustrated entirely by photographs. He produced permanent prints by sensitizing paper with silver nitrate and treating the exposed paper with salt solution. His interests were not confined to photography and, after showing his academic brilliance at an early age, he continued throughout his life his studies in such subjects as mathematics, chemistry, classics, philosophy, archaeology and Assyriology.

The Fox Talbot Museum, housed in a sixteenth-century barn at the Abbey gates, stands as a memorial to his achievements. Converted into a museum in 1975 by the use of massive oak and elm timbers, the ground floor consists of a record and explanation of Fox Talbot's family life and his achievements in photography and other subjects. On the upper floor an exhibition gallery houses a series of exhibitions on photography from Fox Talbot's time to the latest developments.

The oriel window in the South Gallery of the Abbey – a copy of the earliest extant Fox Talbot 'photogenic drawing'.

Photoportrait of William Fox Talbot taken by John Moffat of Edinburgh in 1866.

Markets and Fairs

The solid market cross has found a resting place today in the children's playground of the school. Its various sites in the village represent seven hundred years of the right to hold a weekly market which Ela obtained for the villagers in the 1240s. The earliest markets were held in the wide space in front of the church, but they were later moved to the High Street. As late as 1747 the Bath Journal states that '*whereas the town of Lacock has a very flourishing cornmarket, from 3 April will begin and continue a weekly market for the sale of fat or lean cattle, sheep and swine*'. The tithe barn was then used as a market hall.

But Ela, founder of the Abbey, also procured the privilege of an annual fair for the village '*on the vigil, feast and morrow of St Thomas*'. This occasion for celebration and jolly revelry is one that has survived. If its date has moved during the centuries – at times been eclipsed – it has now settled on the August Bank Holiday. Stalls and sideshows abound, quaint costume and masks are donned, and with a spirit of cheerful delight near neighbours and visitors are entertained.

The 18th-century lock-up for drunks and disorderlies in East Street, rebuilt for the Trust by the local Stonemason in the 1950s.

The Village Hall stall at the Folk Festival.

The High Street celebrates.